All about India

Introduction to India for Kids

By

Shalu Sharma

Copyright:

Disclaimer:

Other books by the author

India For Kids: Amazing Facts About India

Hinduism For Kids: Beliefs And Practices

Religions of the World for Kids

Hindi Language For Kids And Beginners: Speak Hindi Instantly

Hinduism Made Easy: Hindu Religion, Philosophy and Concepts

Mahatma Gandhi For Kids And Beginners

Mother Teresa of Calcutta: Finding God Helping Others: Life of Mother Teresa

Life and Works of Aryabhata

Travel India: Enjoying India to the Fullest: Things to do in India

Facts About Tigers - For Kids

Travel Delhi: Places to Visit in Delhi

Table of contents

Introduction to India

The history of India dates back thousands of years to the B.C. era. Archaeological evidence has already proven that humans were alive in India all the way back in 30,000 B.C. It is very easy to be fascinated by India because it is made up of so much history, buildings, people and cultures. In fact many people don't realize this, but India is one of the most multicultural countries in the world. There are several regional languages spoken in the country and over 122 unofficial languages and 1600 dialects. There are 22 national languages in India including English, but most of the communication surrounding government and business is used in Hindi and English. This has helped India become a globalized country where they can do business internationally with foreign businesses. While this has helped improve the nation's economy, the country still remains a very poor country with millions of people struggling to survive.

India is a subcontinent of Asia in the south, but is separated from the rest of the continent by the continental wall located in the Himalayas. Of course the country still gets a lot of travelers and immigrants entering the country from its surrounding Asian countries. The landscape of India is very diverse, just like the people and the cultures there. You will find a great amount of mountain ranges, national parks, deserts, beaches, and forests across the regions of the country. This diversity stems from the position of the continent and the various climates that Indian regions fall under. In a way, you could compare the country's landscape to that of the United States because they also have mountains, deserts, forests and beaches throughout the country as well. But in India, their regional landscapes have actually helped shaped the cultures in those areas.

The auto-rickshaw is a popular mode of transport in India

If you were to look at a map of the world then you could easily find India because its land mass sticks right out into the water. The southern end of India is actually a peninsula. It is surrounded by three seas and the Indian Ocean lies south of them. India currently has seven union territories and twenty nine states. The governmental system of law in the country is very similar to the American system of law. The Government of India, also known as the Central Government or Union Government, is the country's federal government. They are the governing authority over the country's union territories and states. However, these territories and states also have their own governing bodies as well. It is similar to how America has state and local governments in addition to the federal government. India and its states even have three branches of government; legislative, judicial and executive. The center of the union government is located in the capital of the country, which is New Delhi. The city is also a huge tourist attraction and it contains many international business and franchises such as McDonald's, Pizza Hut, Xerox, Kodak, Coca Cola and General Motors. If you plan on visiting India in the near future then you will be overwhelmed by both the similarities and differences between this country and yours.

Capital of India

The capital of India is New Delhi, or just Delhi. This city seats all the branches of the Indian government, which are the judiciary, legislative and executive branches. It also holds the Government of the National Capital Territory of Delhi. This is the governing authority that oversees the laws and regulations surrounding the eleven districts of Delhi. The city of Delhi has a total population of about 13 million people and the entire metropolitan area has about 23 million people.

Humayun's Tomb in Delhi, the capital of India

Delhi was not always the capital of India. The country has actually had over a dozen capitals since the beginning of its existence. The last capital of India was Calcutta (renamed as Kolkata), which was during the British Raj (rule) of

Indian history. The British Raj was a period between 1858 and 1947 when the British ruled over India. Some people in those days referred to it as British India. In 1911, King George V decided to transfer the official capital of India from Calcutta to the city of Delhi. This was at the climax of the Imperial Durbar, which was a mass assembly that marked the succession of King George V from his late father King Edward VII.

Delhi already had a long history in India. Before it was proclaimed as the official capital of India, Delhi was already the financial and political center throughout several ancient Indian empires. The city was located in the northern region of the country, which is near the borders of its surrounding countries. The British administration during this time felt that it would be easier to regulate the country from Delhi rather than from Calcutta, which lies on the eastern coast of the country.

When India gained its independence from the United Kingdom in 1947, a special district called "New Delhi" was created inside the city of Delhi. People now refer to Delhi as a union territory. In 1991, the Indian government passed the 69th amendment to their constitution which declared Delhi to be officially known as the National Capital Territory of Delhi. In other words, this is the territory where the capital is located. The actual capital, New Delhi, lies inside of the territory. Delhi has remained the capital of India ever since 1911 and there are currently no plans for this to change by the Indian government any time soon. The name New Delhi was given in 1927.

You will also find McDonalds in India. The prices are in Indian Rupees

Today, New Delhi is a popular tourist attraction that brings millions of travelers from around the world every year. With all the rich history of India, there are many museums built in the capital to glorify the main events that have happened in the country. Some of the museums include National Gallery of Modern Art, Indira Gandhi Memorial Museum, National Rail Museum, and the Supreme Court of India Museum. There was recently an announcement that the National War Memorial and Museum was going to be constructed in New Delhi within the next few years. Besides the museums and historical sites, the capital is filled with beautifully landscaped gardens and parks for tourists to walk through.

People of India

There are about 1.25 billion people that reside in the country of India. This makes it the second most populated nation in the entire world, and right behind China which has 1.35 billion people.

People at the Taj Mahal in the city of Agra

The people of India are spread out across different regions of the country into regional ethno linguistic groups. This is due to India's history of immigration and foreign rule, like from Britain, over their people. The diversity also stems from different climates, religions, and cultures. India is a very culturally diverse country and contains people who speak many different languages. Unlike most other countries that only have one or two common languages, India has numerous regional languages and 22 official languages spoken by its people. One official language, Hindi, is spoken in the north and other official language,

English, is used for business and governmental purposes. The Indian Constitution has officially recognized 15 regional languages throughout the country. These languages are Bengali, Assamese, Hindi, Gujarati, Malayalam, Kannada, Marathi, Kashmiri, Punjabi, Oriya, Tamil, Sindhi, Sanskrit, Urdu, and Telugu. However, there are also over 1,500 other unofficial languages and dialects used by people throughout India as well. Most of these are tribal languages that don't have too many outside followers, so the India Constitution does not officially recognize them.

An Indian wedding

The Constitution of India states that all citizens have equal rights. However the country used to have a rigid caste system for quite a long time which is still prevalent to some extent. A caste system is basically a type of social stratification that separates people in to groups based on income, wealth, occupation and social status. These groups were referred to as either castes or jatis. In 1901, there were over 1600 caste groups on record in India. But as the country gained more independence and built a better democracy, the caste system began to break apart in the cities. Unfortunately, the rural areas of India have some form of the caste system which still exists. Even though this is against the Constitution of India, the Union Government doesn't have the resources to enforce all of the laws in every rural area of the country. So the people who live in these areas pretty much have to fend for themselves. The same goes for their food, clothing and shelter as well. On the upside, the rural townspeople lookout for each other and stick together like a tribe.

Can you see Indian women wearing the traditional sari (saree)?

The people of India take spirituality very seriously. Even though they are diverse in their religions and languages, the majority still earn for a connection with the spiritual world. In order to make this connection they pray, mediate, sing, dance and celebrate. In fact the Indian people love to play all types of music to connect to the spirits such as Hindi songs from film movies, pop, folk, R&B and classical music. India actually has two forms of music that are popular in the northern and southern regions of the country. Hindustani music is played a lot in the north and Carnatic music is played a lot in the south. The music is a form of both cultural expression and spiritual inspiration to everyone who hears it. This is how the Indian people of all socioeconomic classes are able to deal with their problems and find peace in their lives.

Ancient history of India

The ancient history of India can be traced through archaeological evidence all the way back to about 75,000 years ago. As for the earliest recorded civilization, there are scriptures that date all the way back to 3300 B.C. This civilization was known as the Indus Valley Civilization, which existed in northwest India and throughout present day Pakistan. Then during the Mature Harappan period of 2600 B.C., this civilization began to get technologically advanced by developing an urban centre. However this civilization eventually collapsed around 1900 B.C., and was eventually followed by what is known as the Iron Age Vedic Civilization. This civilization resided throughout the North Indian River Plain, or what is historically known as the Indo-Gangetic Plain. They were the ones that first developed a political territory, and it was governed by sixteen kingdoms. This rise in political power in northern India was known as the Mahajanapadas.

A portrait of Buddha

One of the most notable figures in Ancient Indian history came around 600 B.C. This was the famous teacher known as Buddha. Some other names he was called were Siddhartha Gautama, Gautama Buddha and Shakyamuni. But in general, people just refer to him as Buddha. The name "Buddha" means the enlightened one or the awakened one. He is recognized for teaching people how to end their suffering by not giving into cravings or ignorance. The religion of Buddhism was formed as a result of Buddha's teachings. It is one of the oldest religions in the world and is still practiced even to this day. Buddhism is a religion without any particular God. The people who study the words of Buddhism are not praying to him like a God. They are simply referring to him as the enlightened one who was given the proper knowledge from the spiritual world to teach others about how to live a better life.

The Taj Mahal

By the time the 4th century B.C. came around, the Indian subcontinent was ruled by the Maurya Empire. This was around the time that Pali and Prakrit literature started getting written in northern India and Sangam literature began getting written in southern India. As the Maurya Empire began to fade out near the end of the 3rd century, the Middle Kingdoms of India took over the country. These were a series of separate kingdoms that ruled various regions of India for the next 1,500 years. This was the period that the Hindu religion really began to spread across the country and gain more popularity with the average Indian citizen. Historians refer to this period of Indian history as the Golden Age of India. This was when various Indian cultures, religions, administrations and customs were introduced to new parts of Asia. It even got to a point where kingdoms in southern India began to do business with the Roman Empire, which occurred around 70 A.D.

This allowed Indian cultural influences to spread throughout Southeast Asia and beyond. Over the next 2000 years, India had been conquered and ruled by a number of Asian and Middle Eastern empires. It eventually got to the point where the British ruled the country as well. It was only within the last 65 plus years that India finally gained its independence from foreign rule.

Modern history of India

India has been through a lot of changes in the last 100 years. One of the most notable Indian leaders was Mahatma Gandhi. He was one of the most influential figures in modern Indian history because he was able to successfully help India gain its independence from the British. During the 16th and 17th centuries, many European trading companies came to India to do business and competed viciously against each other. This English trading in India continued onward all the way to the 18th century. What ended up happening was the English businesses dominated over all of the traditional Indian marketplaces and caused many natives to lose their businesses. At this point, the British became the dominating power in India and used their money and influence to gain control over the country. With the British influence over India, they administered revolutionary changes to the Indian way of life. These changes affected the political, economic and social way of life in the country.

The India Gate in Delhi is a popular tourist attraction

During the 19th century, the British government brought more of their troops and political figures to the country. This was when India's natural resources began being used for commercial exploitation. Not only were the resources being exploited, but the Indian people's labor was being exploited as well. This created great tension between the Indian people and the British imperialists who were regulating the country. By the end of the 19th century in 1885, a middle class group of Indian people got together and created the Indian National Congress with Allan Octavian Hume, a civil servant and a political reformer. This was a public organization that became influential towards the Indian Independence Movement. Of course the Indian people did not obtain independence right away, but this was the beginning of a decades' long journey to get that freedom and independence from the British government.

Mahatma Gandhi is the Father of the nation

The turning point in the anti-British mass movement was when a man named Mahatma Gandhi joined the Indian Independence Movement. He became a central leader in this movement and taught other people to use resistance through non-violent methods in order to obtain their civil rights. Not only did this encourage other Indians to follow in his footsteps, but it encouraged independence movements for civil rights all across the world as well. The British did not respond well to the Indians' stubbornness toward their leadership, but as the years passed they eventually came to the conclusion that they had no more influence over the Indian people. After numerous Indian campaigns demanding independence, the British eventually left India in the year 1947. This was the year that India finally got their freedom. It was also the year that Pakistan became a separate nation from British India. Unfortunately the leader of the Indian Independence movement, Gandhi, was assassinated in 1948. But he did get to live long enough to see India finally gain its independence from the British.

For the last 65 years, India has been known as the Republic of India or Bharat. But even though they became independent, they still faced many territorial disputes with their neighboring countries, like China and Pakistan. There were many wars because of these disputes, such as the Sino-Indian War and the several Indo-Pakistan wars. Eventually these wars settled down (but the border dispute still exist) and India began to rise as an economic and political power. Military analysts across the world believe that India could eventually become a more powerful country in the near future.

Culture of India

India is a very multicultural country. The Indian people take their culture very seriously. The things that make up their culture include religion, language, music, dance, food and architecture. However all of these things are not the same throughout the entire country. In fact, they are greatly diversified in these because of its varied people who live there. India is broken up into many different states and each one has their own unique culture. The culture of a region is primarily influenced by the religion and climate of the region. Not only that, the historical background of India has greatly influenced the existing cultures of the country. Since the history of the country dates back thousands of years, the traditions that existed back have been carried over to the present. The majority of these traditions are derived from religion. If you look at all the Indian festivals, like the Karthigai festival, you will see that there are religious undertones to the event. These festivals are usually honoring some kind of God or spiritual influence in the lives of the people. The festivals of Divali (festival of light) and Holi (festival of colors) too both have cultural and religious significance. The Hindu religion usually has the most festivals that pertain to worshipping the good over evil.

A traditional Indian musical show

The varying climates of India have created different kinds of wildlife. The country is rich with exotic wildlife, and these animals have a great impact on the Indian culture. The word "wilderness" is referred to as "jungle" in India. This is where the word originated from. It is also the basis for the book entitled "The Jungle Book," which is set in India as well. There are many stories and fables told regarding the animals of India. Even in religion, certain animals are viewed differently than others. For example, the Hindus revere cows because they see them as a symbol of non-violence and good fortune. For this reason, you will find wild and domestic cows walking the streets of India without their owners watching them. In addition, in some states there are certain laws that say that cows cannot be butchered and consumed as beef. It is also a religious custom to keep cows safe.

This is "chaat" a popular street food

Food is probably one of the most important aspects of any culture. Food can really tell you about a particular culture by studying the ingredients that are used and the way it is prepared. Since India is very diverse, this means their cuisines are diverse as well. The food is influenced by both the religion and climate of the region in which it is prepared. Therefore you will find vegetarian dishes, meat dishes, spices, salads, desserts, chapattis and much more. India has even become more westernized with their food by allowing western franchises, like McDonald's and Pizza Hut, to open up shop in their big cities. Of course the menu choices are a little different to cater to the most popular Indian cultures and their food preferences. You will not find ham or beef burgers in these fast food joints.

Finally, the clothing in India is diverse due to the local culture and geography of the region. However you will typically find women wearing a sari, which is a draped garment that goes over the body. The salwar kemeez is also very popular amongst Indian women. As for the men, they will typically wear a traditional waist garment that is called a lungi or dhoti. Many Indians wear handmade clothes that are stitched together from cotton material called khadi.

Western clothing is now normal in India. A lot of items are handmade in India by poor families who try to sell their creations on the streets and make money. Some of these creations include bangles, earrings, finger rings and more. These items are not just something to wear. They give you a real sense of the culture and lifestyle of the person who made them.

Religions of India

Religious beliefs are very diverse in India because of all the different cultures and ethnic groups that live there. But the two most popular religions in India are Islam and Hinduism. Statistics show that 80% of the Indian population is made up of Hindus and only 15% is made up of Muslims. The other minority religions of the country are Buddhism, Sikhism, Jainism and Christianity. The Constitution of India gives everybody in the country the right to freedom of religion. This is a fundamental right for all people in the country, which is why there are so many different religions throughout its regions.

Statues of Lord Ram (in the middle) with wife Sita and brother Lakshman

The ancient religions of India, such as Hinduism, were passed down from thousands of years ago when the ancient civilization known as the Indus Valley Civilization came to exist. They inhabited the northern and western parts of India throughout their existence. It was in these locations that they developed traditions, language and script, worship rituals and spirituality devoted to Hindu beliefs that are still prevalent today. These were also the birthplaces of many Hindu saints.

A Hindu temple

Every year the northern city of Allahabad hosts one of the biggest Hindu festivals in the world, which is called Kumbh Mela. This is where Hindus from around the world travel to this Indian city in order to come together and bathe in the three sacred Indian rivers that pass through here. These three rivers Ganges, Yamuna and Saraswati, come together to form one river. Allahabad is one of the most holy places for the Hindus. Basically the reason why these rivers are so special is because the Hindus believe that their gods once carried a pot of nectar and the nectar fell into the sea after it churned. This means if you bathe in this godly water then it will cleanse you completely of all your sins. In 2013 alone, more than 80 million Hindus came to this festival and bathed in the sacred rivers. Banaras is another very holy place where Hindus like to bathe in the river Ganges. Hindus believe that if they take a dip in this place, it will wash their sins away.

Many Indian religions, like Buddhism and Hinduism, share common traits and customs. For example, they each practice yoga and meditation in order to become closer with the spiritual world. They also believe in reincarnation after you die and trying to achieve karma in the afterlife by being good when you are living your multiple lives. These are Indian spiritual beliefs that are common throughout all the regions of India, and they don't come from just one religion only. In fact these spiritual beliefs have influenced other people all over the world to take up these religious practices and customs. People who want to be reborn into a better life will become kind to others in their present life and not hurt or steal from anybody else. In other words, they are trying to refrain from "sinning" in order to be rewarded in the next life.

India also has the third largest Muslim and Shia population in the entire world. You can find shrines in India devoted to Islamic saints such as Nizamuddin Auliya and Moinuddin Chishti. These shrines also attract Muslim followers from all around the world as well. One famous Islamic piece of architecture that tourists really love is the Qutb Minar and the Taj Mahal. What is even more fascinating is that non-religious people love to come to India just to see these historical religious buildings and monuments, even though they are not associated with the religion. That is the power of the religious history of India.

Other major world religions of India include Sikhism, Jainism, Zoroastrianism and Christianity. If you want to learn more about Hinduism then you might wish to read this book "Hinduism For Kids: Beliefs And Practices" available on Amazon.

Languages of India

Multiculturalism has always been part of Indian life, which has caused many language families to be used by the people. But on a national level, the two official languages of the country are Hindi and English. The original Indian constitution was written in Devanagari script. In this constitution, it declared Hindi to be the nation's official language for the entire country and union. However, the Indian government was also aware that there were many regions in India where people did not speak Hindi.

A road side eatery. Can you see the signs in English and in Hindi?

Due to the legacy of British colonialism in India, English became the official language that was used for business, education and governmental purposes around the country.

Hindi and English are the only two languages that the Indian Parliament will allow in the Constitution of India. The original writers of the Indian constitution did not foresee British colonialism taking place or that English would be actively used throughout most of the country. So if they were alive today they would certainly be shocked to see that English is actively used throughout the country. You will see English on road signs, building signs and other buildings throughout the main cities. Now if you were to go into smaller towns without a lot of tourists then you would find people primarily speaking Hindi to each other.

A sign in both in Hindi and English at the Agra Fort

The Indian languages are broken down into two linguistic families; the Indo-European and the Dravidian. The Indo-European group of languages is spoken by about 75% of the Indian population. This group represents many of the popular European languages such as English, French,

Spanish, Portuguese, and Persian. Statistics show that around 700 million Indians actively speak at least one of these languages. As for the Dravidian language family, about 200 million people speak these languages. The group that speaks these languages mostly exists in southern India. They are comprised of minority languages that most people outside of India have never heard of before. Some of these languages include Konda, Gondi, Tamil, and Malayalam. A few of the languages have spread to Pakistan, Bangladesh and even to Malaysia and Singapore because of immigration. However they are not official languages in any of these countries and are just used by immigrant speakers and their families. But if you were to ask anybody in Europe or in the Americas about these languages, they wouldn't be able to tell you anything about them. They are mostly familiar with Indo-European languages only.

A sign in English

If you ever plan on coming to India then you should just make sure you know English. This is the official government language and you will be able to find your way around just find with this language. Contrary to popular belief amongst foreigners, there is no "Indian" language. The country has so many different religions and dialects that it would be impossible to learn one language that could communicate with everybody in the country. Even if you learn Hindi, you will only be able to communicate with 500 million people in the country. That is actually less than 40% of the total Indian population. Therefore, just stick with English with some Hindi and you will be fine there.

Geography of India

India is a country located in the Asian continent on the eastern side of the world. It is situated just north of the equator and is the 7th largest country in the entire world. More specifically, India is in South Asia and lies mostly on top of the Indian tectonic plate. On the eastern side of the country lies the Bay of Bengal and on the western side is the Arabian Sea. The southern side has the Laccadive Sea, which projects into the Indian Ocean as it goes further south. The Gulf of Mannar and the Palk Strait separates the country from Sri Lanka in the southern region. India also has many islands away from the mainland to the southeast. These are the Nicobar and Andaman Islands. They are located 750 miles from the mainland and share the same maritime boundary with Thailand, Indonesia and Burma. In addition, Lakshadweep is an archipelago of 36 atolls and coral reefs in the Laccadive Sea.

Where do you see Sri Lanka on the map?

India lies entirely on top of the Indian Plate. This tectonic plate was formed when it was originally split from an ancient continent known as Gondwanaland. Scientists believe that up until 200 million years ago, the earth had two big supercontinents; Laurasia and Gondwana. These continents eventually drifted into each other, which caused them to break apart into separate micro continents. This continental collision was what caused the Indian plate to form. The result was Australia and India being split apart from each other. Scientists think that the two subcontinents were actually together at some point in the earth's history, but this is not for sure. If you look at these countries on a map and study the way they are shaped, it almost looks like you could piece them together if it were a jigsaw puzzle. In other words, the shapes indicate the two subcontinents could have been one at some point long ago.

The northern Indian frontiers were the first to ever be explored and settled in the country. These areas are greatly defined by the enormous Himalayan mountain range there. The Himalayan mountain range borders with other Asian countries, such as Nepal, Bhutan and China. In the western border of India, it lies next to Pakistan. The border line goes right through the Thar Desert and Punjab Plain. This northwestern region of India is where all the hotter desert climates are located. But then when you go to the northeastern regions of the country, you have the deeply forested regions that contain the Kachin Hills and Chin Hills. Then along the western and eastern sides of the country, there are plenty of exotic beaches that lookout upon the seas which surround the country.

Geologists believe the Indian Plate continues to move in a northeastern direction. This means it is actually pushing the Indian subcontinent into the Eurasian Plate that is located just north of it. When plates collide on land like this, it forms mountainous ranges like the Himalayas. In fact, the Himalayas were formed because the Indian continent used to be alone in the ocean and ended up colliding with the Asian continent about 45 million years ago. Even to this day, the continent continues to collide at a collision rate of 2 centimeters per year.

India's neighbor

Many people around the world associate India with the Middle East, but it is geographically a South Asian country. India's biggest neighboring countries consist of China, Pakistan, Afghanistan, Bangladesh and Nepal. The countries to the west of India consist of the Islamic nations that have a huge Muslim population such as Pakistan and Afghanistan. The countries to the east of India contain a bigger Asian population such as China, Bangladesh and Nepal. With all of this diversity surrounding India, this brings a lot of tourism and multiculturalism into the country. It is one of the reasons why India has such a variety of ethnic diversity. Not only does this increase trade opportunities between countries, but it increases the country's tourism trade which benefits the Indian economy in the process.

India has had its history of territorial disputes and wars with a few of its neighbors, particularly China. China is just north of India and its borders run through many Indian states, including Sikkim, Jammu and Kashmir, Uttarakhand, Arunachal Pradesh, and Himachal Pradesh. China is the most populous country in the entire world. They are considered to be the second biggest economic power in the world, with the second being the United States. Surprisingly, the third strongest economic power is India. Even though there are a lot of poor people in the country, there are a small percentage of rich people as well. Not only that, but international businesses have franchised in India and have driven great economic wealth over to the country. This has helped India boost its economy and create more job opportunities for its people. Economists predict that India and China could eventually become the most powerful countries in the world, which just happen to be neighbors in the Asian continent.

Pakistan was once a territory of India, but they were divided by a Partition in the year 1947. This was the same year that India gained its independence from Britain. Pakistan, which lies to the west of India, is now its own country and is separate from India. In the beginning of their independence, the two countries had a lot of territorial disputes over the borderlines that separate them apart. A civil war broke out between the countries, which succeeded in 1971. The country of Bangladesh was formed as a result because it was previously a part of Pakistan. The country now shares their borders with the Indian states of Rajasthan, Gujarat, Jammu and Kashmir, and Punjab. And despite some people thinking Pakistan is a Middle Eastern country, it is technically still a South Asian country. Its coastline lies along the Gulf of Oman and the Arabian Sea. Bangladesh and India share a very large border.

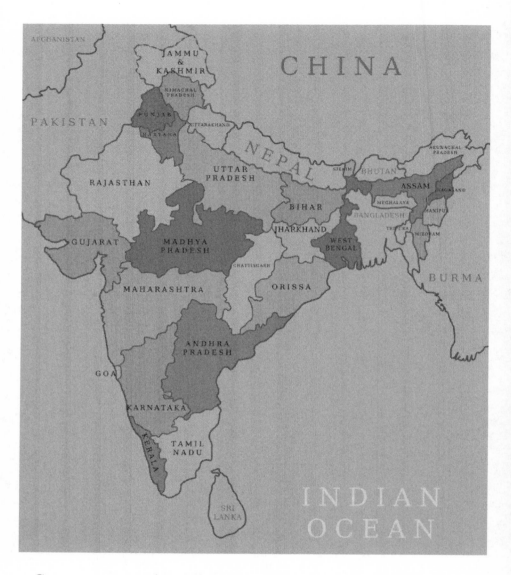

Can you remember all the neighboring countries of India?

The Indian states of Meghalaya, West Bengal, Tripura, Assam and Mizoram all touch the Bangladesh border in the east. When Bangladesh was once part of Pakistan, it went by the name of East Pakistan. But after the civil war in 1971, it got renamed "Bangladesh" and became its own country.

Other bordering countries of India include Kingdom of Bhutan, Union of Myanmar (former Burma), Maldives and Sri Lanka (about 80 km from the southern tip of India).

Festivals of India

Festivals are a big part of the Indian culture and a very important part of people's lives in India. To most people in the world, festivals are just a celebratory event where you put on an entertaining show of some kind and have a good time. But with Indian festivals, they are more related to spirituality and helping people find inner peace. These festivals are often supposed to help people connect to the spiritual world. Also, the festivals remind people of the victory of good over evil. There are all different kinds of festivals related to different religions such as Hinduism, Buddhism, Jainism and Sikhism. One of the most popular festivals is called Diwali. This is a five day festival that signifies the beginning of the Hindu New Year. The Hindus often refer to it as the Festival of Lights because there are fireworks, candles and small clay lamps that all light up the environment. But these lights are not just used because they look pretty. They are a representation of good being victorious over evil and brightness shining down over darkness. In other words, the lights are a symbol of joy and happiness in the eyes of the people who celebrate this event.

Children playing Holi

Another popular festival in India is the Ganesh Chaturthi. This festival is a ten day celebration that falls between August and September of each year. It honors the birth of Lord Ganesha, which is a beloved Hindu god with an elephant head. You can expect to see lots of hand crafted elephant statues at this event, which are all crafted to look like Ganesha. These statues are installed inside homes, podiums, storefronts and right out on the streets. Then after the festival is over, the statues get paraded around on the streets. While the parade is taking place, there is a lot of dancing and singing going on as well. Finally, the statues are placed into the ocean and submerged in the water.

The festival of Durga Puja

The two day festival called Holi is another event that celebrates good being victorious over evil. But instead of using lights, this event uses colors. That is why it is commonly referred to as the Festival of Colors. People at this festival will usually pour colored water and colored powder over each other and have lots of colorful decorated parties. They will also dance over water sprinklers and sing songs. Holi is an event where everyone is carefree and is not afraid to have a good time, even if it means getting dirty and wet. Adults will sometimes even consume a cannabis paste called Bhang, which enhances the colorful experience in their minds by getting high off the cannabis (something that should not be tried). Hindu children play Holi with their friends on the streets and are a lot of fun.

Some other popular festivals of Indian include Navaratri, Durga Puja, Onam, Krishna Janmashtami, Vasant

Panchami, Maha Shivaratri and Rama Navami. Besides the popular festivals that take place in Delhi, Calcutta and other popular cities, villages and towns in India, there are also hundreds of tribal and regional festivals that most people don't hear about. The tribal festivals are usually private events held by tribal followers who are honoring their God or spiritual leaders. It is safe to say that the festivals of India are just as diverse as the religions and people. This is part of what makes India such an exciting place because the events and people are different as you travel throughout the country.

Overview of Indian food

Indian food is very diverse throughout the various regions of India because of all the different ethnic groups and cultures that make up the country. Also, the varying occupations and climates within these regions of the country have a lot of influence over Indian food as well. These differences affect the agriculture of the crops, which in turn influences the food recipes of the cuisines. Therefore, all of the herbs, spices, fruits and vegetables that make up Indian food will be unique in each Indian region. However, these regional foods all have one thing in common. The cuisines were all developed and influenced by Dharmic beliefs. The concept of Dharma has multiple meanings though because all of the main Indian religions see Dharma in a different way. These religions are Buddhism, Hinduism, Jainism and Sikhism.

A plate of Indian food

In the western world, there is no one word translation to describe what dharma means. But when it comes to its influence over Indian food, it generally has to do with the customs and conduct related to people's religious views. One of the most popular examples of this is vegetarianism. Many Hindus are taught to be vegetarians because they view the cow as a sacred animal and a symbol for life, whereas people in the west just see cows as hamburger meat. So if you go to any Hindu restaurants in India then you will likely find a lot of vegetarian meals like rice, tofu vindaloo, samosas, onion bhajis, crispy vegetable pakoras, spicy vegan potato curry and Indian chickpeas.

This is "poha" made of rice. Poha is eaten specially in the morning

Besides religious influences, there are also foreign influences that have shaped the menus of many Indian restaurants around the country. The history of India has proven this after all of the foreign invasions they have had from the British and even from the Portuguese, who were responsible for introducing breadfruit and chili pepper to the Indian people. Now in the 21st century, the western influences of the United States have certainly made an impact on the Indian people. You will now find popular American fast food chains, like McDonalds and Burger King, in big Indian cities such as New Delhi.

Vegetables being sold in the market in India

India has gotten a lot of western cuisine introduced to them by these fast food franchises coming over to their country. But the menus of these restaurants are a little different for the Indian people than they are for the American people. Franchises tend to diversify their menus in order to satisfy the cultural demands of the people they are selling their food to. For example, McDonald's has a burger in India called the McVeggie. This contains potato, peas, carrots and Indian spices all fried together to form a patty that is golden brown. Westerners might think it looks like a chicken patty, but it is actually just a vegetable patty. Now if the McVeggie were to be served in America then it might not go over to well with Americans because they like beef hamburger patties. But since many of the Indian people are vegetarians, McDonald's created a unique burger that would satisfy the cultural demand of a vegetarian public.

Of course, you can still purchase fish and chicken patties, but what you won't find are hamburger patties.

A typical English breakfast. Very few people eat baked beans and hash browns in India

This goes back to the Indian culture's view on the cow being a sacred animal. So as you can see, even restaurants from other countries will still cater to the cultural standards of the Indian people.

What do Indians eat?

If you ever wondered what Indians eat then keep on reading. As far as food is considered in India, there is no simple answer. It may not be as varied as the languages of India but it certainly is a little complex. But food habits of the Indians can be divided into four regional categories; North, South, East and West.

Plate of chapattis

The North Indians prefer to eat wheat in the form of chapattis, nan breads, parathas, puris (fried) and its variants of flat bread with curries which could be meat or vegetables. Daal or pulses are very popular in India and are eaten with rice or chapattis. Rice dishes usually eaten by North Indians will be plain boiled rice, pulau rice or biryanis (vegetables or chicken biryanis). The food prepared are moderately spiced and less hot compared to the South Indians. Yogurt called "curd" in India is used in many dishes in North Indian cuisine. South Indians tend to eat more rice with curry.

Here's a list of types of food Indian's eat. Feel free to try some of these when you are in India. Most likely, you have tried some of them in your local Indian restaurant but trust me the food in India will taste much better. The spices will be better and more fresh although some will find it overwhelming and little spicy.

Chapattis go very well with curries

Chapattis – These are flat bread also known as roti.
Parathas – They are chapattis but are typically fried.
Rice – Rice is very popular. I am sure you must have had rice at home.
Curries – Any type of curry is very popular in India.

Yogurts – Yogurt and curd is very popular in India.

Masala Dosa – A south Indian dish.

Idli and sambar – Another dish popular in India.

Pakodas and bhajis – These are light snacks.

Puris – Puris are small fried Indian bread.

Papads – Pappadums.

Chole bhature – Fried bread served with chick-peas curry.

Kebabs – Roasted or grilled meat.

Pickles - Pickles are very popular and usually taken with the main meal.

Fish – Fish is popular in India partially in the state of West Bengal.

Meat – Meat will usually be in the form of chicken, goat or mutton. You will not find beef or pork in most restaurants in India unless you happen to be in Goa.

Bollywood, the Indian film industry

Bollywood is the nickname for the Indian film industry that uses the Hindi Language. Bollywood is located in city of Mumbai, India. People often misuse the term "Bollywood" by referring it to all Indian cinema. It is just like how people in America often assume that all movies are associated with Hollywood, even though there are plenty of filmmakers around the country who don't even live in Hollywood. So Bollywood just concerns Hindi film cinema only. India itself has a large film industry that goes way beyond just Hindi films. They have films that cater to all of the main national cultures and regional cultures of the country. Some of these cinemas include Haryana, Tamil Nadu, Assam, Punjab and West Bengal; just to name a few. The term "Bollywood" is a nickname that was derived from the center of the American film industry, Hollywood, and the former name of Mumbai known as "Bombay." Mumbai is known as the center of the Hindi film industry. The "B" of Bombay replaced the "H" in Hollywood and so the name became Bollywood. This wasn't the first time that Indian cinema used nicknames like this. The first Indian film cinema nickname was used in 1932 with the name Tollywood, which referred to the Bengal film industry of Tollygunge, Calcutta. The "T" comes from Tollygunge. Tollywood was the inspiration for the name Bollywood.

A scene from Raja Harishchandra (1913), the first Bollywood film produced by Dadasaheb Phalke considered as father of Indian cinema

The first Bollywood film was Raja Harishchandra, which was made in 1913. Of course this was before Bollywood actually got its nickname because it was the beginning of the Hindi film industry. By the 1930s, Indian cinema had produced over 200 films each year. The very first Indian film to have sound was made in 1931, and was called "Alam Ara." This film was a huge success in the country because of the sound addition that nobody had heard in a film before. This inspired Bollywood filmmakers to produce musicals and talkie films.

A music show based on songs from Bollywood movies

Other regional film industries started getting developed throughout India and they also used sound as well. During the 1930s and 1940s, India went through a lot of bad times. There was World War II, the Great Depression, and the Indian independence movement. These tough social topics ended up being the plots of a lot of Indian films throughout this era and it helped people mentally escape their real life problems by watching these films.

Throughout the decades following World War II, Indian cinema was influenced greatly by Western pop culture. Indian films were even considered in international film festivals and award shows. After the Hindi film "Neecha Nagar" had been awarded the Grand Prize at the very first Cannes Film Festival, this put Hindi films on the map. This gained Hindi films more popularity amongst international movie lovers and made Bollywood a name synonymous with Indian films.

A Bollywood movie on TV

In modern times, Bollywood is more popular than ever thanks to the internet. A newer generation of international movie lovers gets to experience Hindi films on YouTube, Amazon and a variety of other video streaming websites. People can now discover older Hindi films that were never released in their own country before. The most popular actor in Bollywood is considered to be Shahrukh Khan. He has appeared in more than 80 Bollywood films and his career has spanned over almost 30 years.

Basic Hindi

Here are some basic Hindi words, phrases and sentences that you can use with someone who knows Hindi well. Remember not all Indians speak Hindi. People from the northern parts of India generally will speak Hindi while from the South won't.

A sign at the Taj Mahal both in Hindi and in English

Hello – Namaste
Welcome – Swagat
You are welcome here – Aap ka swagat hai
My name is Bobby – Mera naam Bobby hai
What is your name? – Aap ka kya naam hai?
Where are you from? – Aap kaha se hai?
I am from USA – Mai USA se hu
What do you do? – Aap kya karte hai?

How are you? – Aap kaise hai?
I am fine – Mai thik hu
And you? – Aur aap?
Cha- Tea
Would you like tea? – Kya aap chai piyenge?
Today – Aaaj
Tomorrow – Kal
Mummy – Ma
Daddy – Pitha
Brother – Bhai
Sister – Bahen
Time – Samay
Home – Ghar
I am going home – Mai ghar jaa raha hu (boy); Mai ghar jaa rahi hu (girl)
Would you like to go to the cinema? – Kya aap cinema chalenge?
Friend – Dost
You are my friend – Tum mera dost ho
Let's go – Chalo
Yes – Haa
No – Nahi
Thank you – Dhanevad
Good – Accha
See you later – Phir milenge
Goodbye – Alvida
One – Ek
Two – Doo
Three – Teen
Four- Char
Five – Panch
Six – Chhaai
Seven – Saath
Eight – Aath
Nine – Nau
Ten – Dus

Quiz questions on India

Here are some questions that you should be able to answer. If you can't remember then go back to the chapters and find the answers.

An Indian instrument called the "table"

1. On which continent is India?
2. India is also known as what?
3. What is the capital of India?
4. Where was the capital before New Delhi?
5. Who ruled India before 1947?
6. How many official languages are there in India?
7. What is the current population of India?
8. What is the ancient civilization of India called?
9. What does Buddha mean?

10. What was the real name of Buddha?

11. Who was Mahatma Gandhi?

12. Name two garments worn by Indian women?

13. Name two garments worn by Indian men?

14. Which animal Hindus consider sacred?

15. Name 4 religions that exist in India?

16. Name one Indian river?

17. What do you think yoga is about?

18. Which script was the Indian constitution originally written in?

19. Indian languages are broken down into two linguistic families. Can you remember which ones?

20. Can you name four neighbors of India?

21. Name one desert in India?

22. Can you name some Indian festivals?

23. Can you name one Indian island?

24. Which festival is the Festival of lights?

25. Which festival is the Festival of colors?

26. Name three types of Indian food?

27. What is the name given to the Indian film industry?

28. How do you say hello in Hindi?

Thank you

Thank you for buying this book. Hope you liked it? I do hope these Hindi words and phrases weren't difficult. I know learning a language can be hard but if you try hard enough, I am sure you will get there.

If you want to learn more Hindi then feel free to get in touch here http://www.shalusharma.com/contact and I will get back to you with more words and phrases.

If you liked this book then feel free to like my Facebook page so that you can keep an eye on new releases: https://www.facebook.com/shalusharmabooks.

If you are thinking of visiting India then you can read travel tips and information on India on my website http://www.shalusharma.com.

Here are some of my other books that you might wish to consider reading.

India For Kids: Amazing Facts About India

Hinduism For Kids: Beliefs And Practices

Religions of the World for Kids

Hindi Language For Kids And Beginners: Speak Hindi Instantly

Hinduism Made Easy: Hindu Religion, Philosophy and Concepts

Mahatma Gandhi For Kids And Beginners

Mother Teresa of Calcutta: Finding God Helping Others: Life of Mother Teresa

Life and Works of Aryabhata

Travel India: Enjoying India to the Fullest: Things to do in India

Facts About Tigers - For Kids

Travel Delhi: Places to Visit in Delhi

Thank you and Namaste
***

Made in the USA
Middletown, DE
22 February 2017